# Cactus Café

**A Story of the Sonoran Desert**

*For Roland and Betsy, Jennifer and Dillon* — K.Z.

*For Anna and Claire* — P.M.

Text copyright ©1997 Kathleen Weidner Zoehfeld.
Book copyright © 1997 Trudy Corporation, 353 Main Avenue, Norwalk, CT 06851.

Soundprints is a division of Trudy Corporation, Norwalk, Connecticut.

Book Design: Shields & Partners, Westport, CT

First Edition 1997
10 9 8 7 6
Printed in China

*Acknowledgments:*
   Our very special thanks to Barbara French of Bat Conservation International, Inc., for her review and guidance.
   Paul Mirocha thanks the Thursday Art Group for their assistance with the art: Anne Gondor, Rhod Lauffer, Diane Lauffer, Ken Matesich, Anna Mirocha, and Gerald Tawaventiwa.


*Library of Congress Cataloging-in-Publication Data*

Zoehfeld, Kathleen Weidner.

Cactus café : a story of the Sonoran Desert / by Kathleen Weidner Zoehfeld ; illustrated by Paul Mirocha.
            p.        cm.
Summary: Describes the activities of various animals living in the Sonoran Desert and their dependence on the saguaro cactus for sustenance.
        ISBN 1-56899-425-7 (hardcover)    ISBN 1-56899-426-5 (pbk.)
1. Desert ecology — Sonoran Desert — Juvenile literature. [1. Sonoran Desert,
2. Desert ecology.   3. Ecology.   4. Desert animals.   5. Saguaro.   6. Cactus.]
I. Mirocha, Paul, ill.    II. Title.

QH104.5.S58Z64 1996                                              96-39092
577.54'09791'7 — dc21                                                CIP
                                                                     AC

# Cactus Café

## A Story of
## the Sonoran Desert

by Kathleen Weidner Zoehfeld
Illustrated by Paul Mirocha

Not a drop of rain has fallen for months. The afternoon sun hammers the dry soil, making the air above it shimmer.

On a rocky hillside, the saguaro cactuses stand like soldiers with their arms upraised. One great saguaro towers above the others. Higher than a two-story house, this giant has been growing for almost two hundred years.

It is nearly summer in the Sonoran Desert of southern Arizona. Most animals are huddled in their nests, hiding from the relentless sun.

A pair of Gila woodpeckers has pecked out a hollow in one of the great saguaro's arms. Snuggled safely inside, their newly-hatched babies peep for food.

Early this morning the father pried two beetles out of the branch of a nearby paloverde tree for them. But still they chirp for more. He stands in his doorway and pants in the heat. The babies will have to wait until the sun is lower.

Out on the horizon, mountains rise purple against the dazzling blue sky. There, in the cool shelter of a cave, sleeps a flock of long-nosed bats.

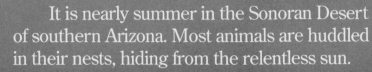

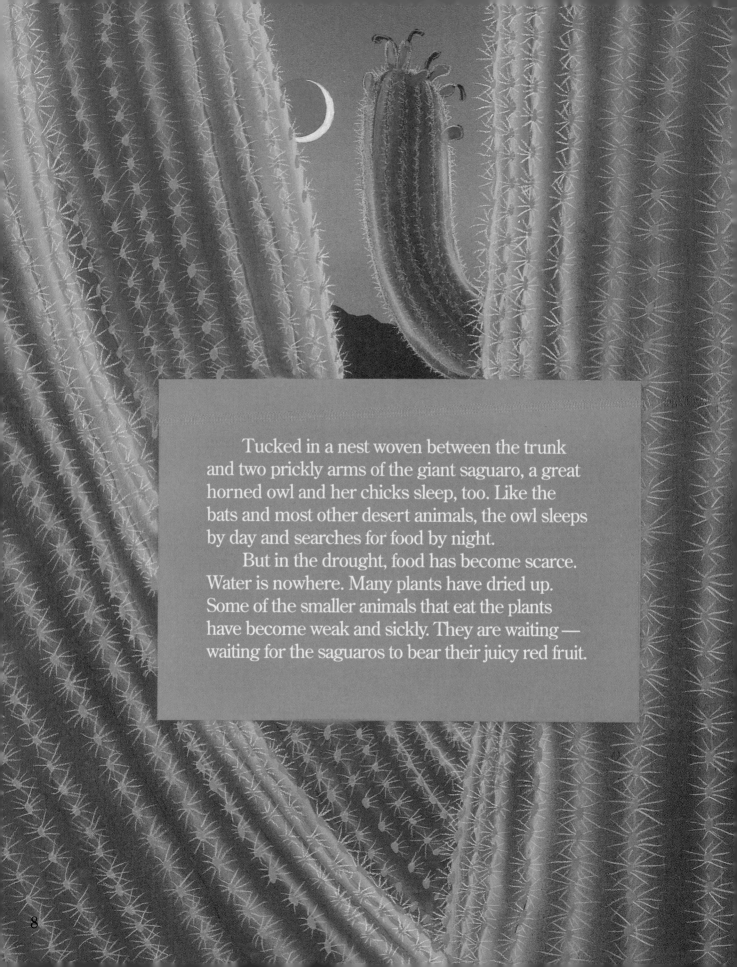

Tucked in a nest woven between the trunk
and two prickly arms of the giant saguaro, a great
horned owl and her chicks sleep, too. Like the
bats and most other desert animals, the owl sleeps
by day and searches for food by night.

But in the drought, food has become scarce.
Water is nowhere. Many plants have dried up.
Some of the smaller animals that eat the plants
have become weak and sickly. They are waiting —
waiting for the saguaros to bear their juicy red fruit.

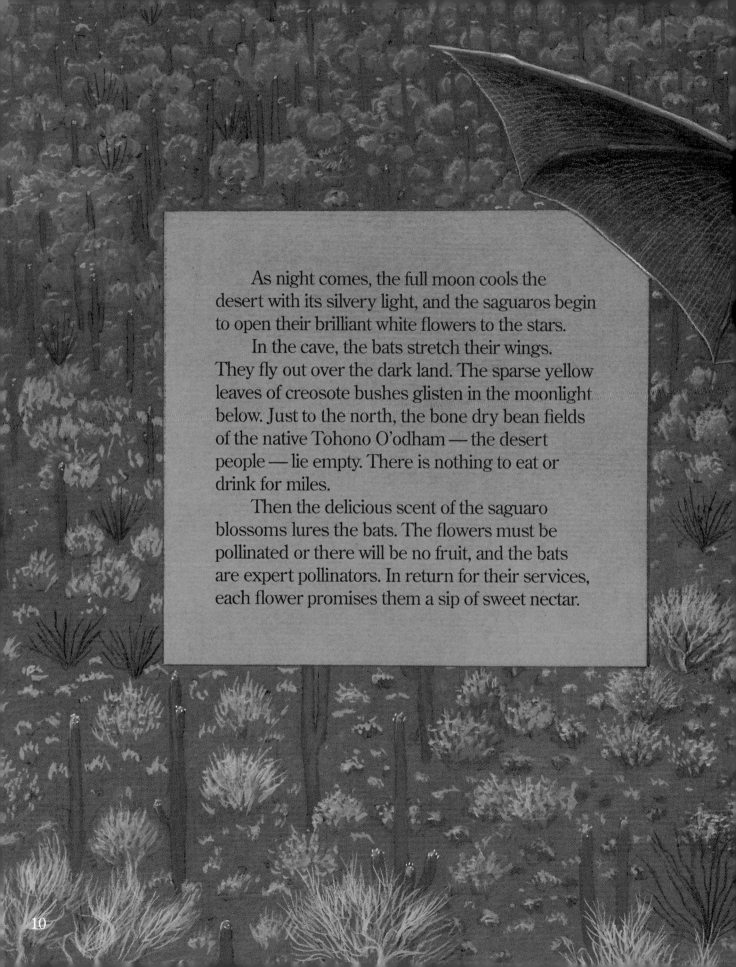

As night comes, the full moon cools the desert with its silvery light, and the saguaros begin to open their brilliant white flowers to the stars.

In the cave, the bats stretch their wings. They fly out over the dark land. The sparse yellow leaves of creosote bushes glisten in the moonlight below. Just to the north, the bone dry bean fields of the native Tohono O'odham — the desert people — lie empty. There is nothing to eat or drink for miles.

Then the delicious scent of the saguaro blossoms lures the bats. The flowers must be pollinated or there will be no fruit, and the bats are expert pollinators. In return for their services, each flower promises them a sip of sweet nectar.

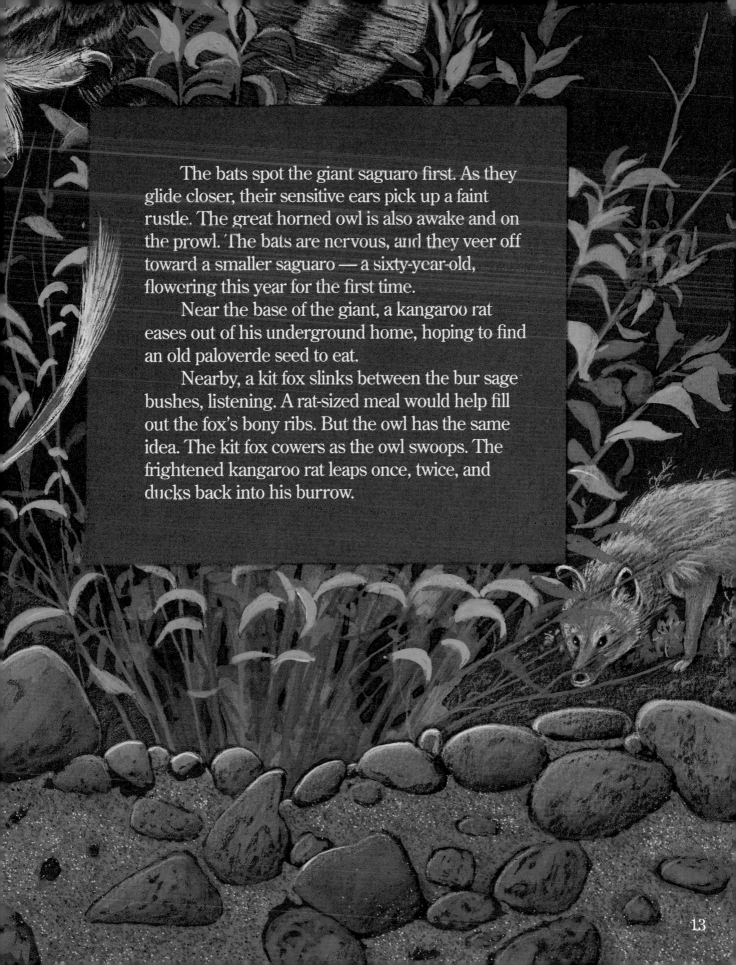

The bats spot the giant saguaro first. As they glide closer, their sensitive ears pick up a faint rustle. The great horned owl is also awake and on the prowl. The bats are nervous, and they veer off toward a smaller saguaro — a sixty-year-old, flowering this year for the first time.

Near the base of the giant, a kangaroo rat eases out of his underground home, hoping to find an old paloverde seed to eat.

Nearby, a kit fox slinks between the bur sage bushes, listening. A rat-sized meal would help fill out the fox's bony ribs. But the owl has the same idea. The kit fox cowers as the owl swoops. The frightened kangaroo rat leaps once, twice, and ducks back into his burrow.

The owl perches atop the giant saguaro and waits. Perhaps hunger will drive the kangaroo rat out of his home again. But the kangaroo rat's burrow has many doors. He follows a long tunnel underground and slips out the back, unnoticed.

Finally the owl sees a small gopher snake winding over the soil. The owl dives and hooks it in her talons.

She carries the wriggling serpent to her nest. While she struggles to feed bits of snake to her babies, the bats return, feeling safer now that the owl is busy.

The bats circle the giant. Then, like hummingbirds, they hover over the blossoms. They push their long noses inside and lap up the nectar with their long tongues. They are polite, taking turns, one to a flower.

Pollen powders the bats' heads and shoulders. As they drink nectar from the blossoms, they deliver grains of pollen from one flower to the next. Hidden inside each saguaro flower, tiny pouches, called ovules, wait to receive the pollen.

The bats drink until their bellies stick out, round as Ping-Pong balls. Stuffed, they hang by their toes from the branches of the paloverde tree. They comb their fur with their toe-claws and eat the leftover pollen.

As the bats lick their wings clean for the night, a noisy group of javelinas snuffles around the giant saguaro, nipping off cactus seedlings and munching them down, spines and all.

In the distance a hungry coyote yodels. The javelinas lift their heads and listen. Another coyote song echoes the first. The javelinas trot to safety under a clump of ironwood trees.

The bats go on licking their wings, untroubled —up out of coyotes' reach. Their only enemy now is the sun, and before it rises they retreat to their mountain cave.

20

Then, as the bats hang from their cave walls and drowse — as snakes and kangaroo rats, owls and javelinas return to their shady homes for the day, the saguaro flowers start to close. Deep inside the flowers, the minute pollen grains inch down tiny tubes toward the ovules.

Wherever a grain of pollen from one flower unites with the ovule of another, a saguaro-seed forms. Around the seeds, the green oval fruits begin to grow.

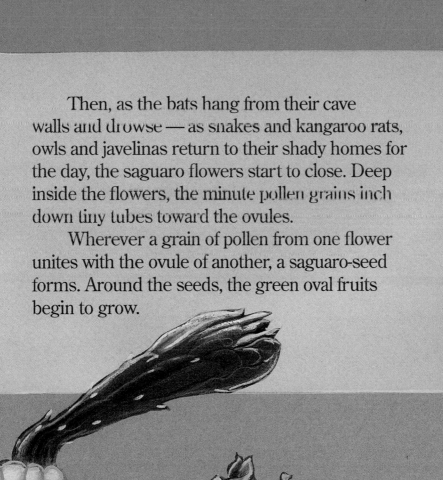

In a few weeks, ruby-red jewels crown the
great cactus and those around it — the saguaro
fruits have ripened!

At last the time has come to feast. The Gila
woodpeckers tear off pieces of juicy red fruit
and return triumphantly to their hungry chicks.
White-winged doves and curve-billed thrashers
perch on the saguaro's arms and dip their beaks
into the moist, melony fruit.

In the shade of the giant, a Tohono O'odham
family sets up camp. For many days, they share
in the harvest, using long, saguaro-rib poles
to reach the tops of the highest cactuses.

As night falls, woodrats, pocket mice, and javelinas wander far from their homes, dining on the fruit that has fallen. Owls, kit foxes, and coyotes stalk them silently, enjoying better hunting — and the saguaro fruit for dessert!

While the animals savor their long-awaited feast, the bats return to circle the giant saguaro. They dip down and taste the fruit briefly. But now the stiletto-leafed agave bushes lure them away. The agave stalks have shot up high and are covered with white blossoms.

The bats dive for agave nectar. Their work of pollinating the majestic saguaros is done — the desert is alive and bursting with sweet, red fruit.

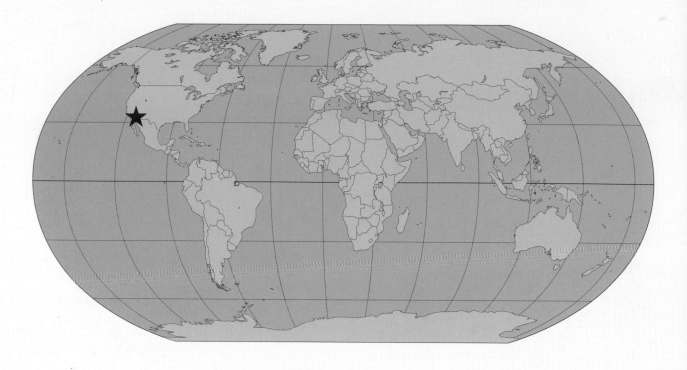

## Sonoran Desert

Long-nosed bats can be found in the Sonoran Desert in southern Arizona. On average, the Sonoran Desert gets less than 6 inches of rain a year. In the summer, temperatures can be over 100°F (37°C).

# About the Sonoran Desert

The Sonoran Desert stretches across most of southern Arizona, the Mexican state of Sonora, and parts of southeastern California and the Baja peninsula. Like all deserts, the Sonoran is a very dry environment. Parts of the western section get less than two inches of rain a year. Only a few plants and animals are tough enough to withstand such parched conditions!

The northeastern part of the desert gets about twelve inches of rain a year. That's a lot of rain for a desert, and the Sonoran Desert supports some of the most spectacular cactus communities in the world. The great saguaro cactus grows only in the Sonoran Desert.

The Sanborn's long-nosed bat is vital to the saguaro's survival. The bats are one of the cactuses' chief pollinators, ensuring the production of millions of new saguaro seeds each year. Even so, it can take a saguaro ten years to grow just a couple of inches, and it must survive for at least 60 years before it can produce its first flower and bear its first fruit. A forest of saguaros can take nearly a century to mature. But if allowed to flourish, a saguaro community makes life in the desert possible for a wide variety of animals. The cactuses' prickly trunks and arms provide shelter and safety, and their flowers and fruit are an essential source of moisture and food.

In recent decades, the biggest threat to the Sonoran Desert has been humans. More people now live in the desert than ever before. Ancient cactus forests are bulldozed in minutes to make room for new homes, roads, and agricultural fields. The saguaro cactuses, the bats, and other animals that depend on them, are in danger. Today, people in Mexico and the United States are working together to preserve this fragile environment.

# Glossary

*Gopher Snake*

*Palo Verde Tree*

*Great Horned Owl*

*Pocket Mouse*

*Kangaroo Rat*

*Sanborne's Long-nosed Bat*

*Kit Fox*

*White-winged Dove*

 Curve-billed Thrasher

 Mesquite Tree

 Gila Woodpecker

 Ocotillo

 Ironwood Tree

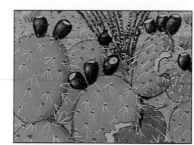 Prickly Pear Cactus

 Javelina

 Saguaro Cactus